Holidays Around the World

Celebrate
Kwanzaa

Carolyn Otto
Consultant, Keith A. Mayes, Ph.D.

NATIONAL GEOGRAPHIC
WASHINGTON, D.C.

candles

∧ A kinara

We celebrate Kwanzaa from December 26 through January 1. Each day we join our friends and families to light a special candle. We think about what it means to be part of the black community, in America and in the world. We celebrate our ancestry.

community

< A young girl leaps into joyous dance in celebration of Kwanzaa at the American Museum of Natural History in New York City.

∧ The Jeter family

ancestry

Kwanzaa was created in 1966 during the black power movement to honor African-American people, our struggles in the United States, our heritage, and our culture. The name Kwanzaa means "first fruits" of the harvest.

During Kwanzaa, we gather together to give thanks for the harvest, which brings us the good things of the earth. We remember the past and our ancestors, who worked the earth. We celebrate hope and promise for the year to come.

> *In the Ethiopian Highlands,
> a girl carries a bundle of wheat.*

We celebrate
the harvest.

We say, "Jambo!"

A Masaii warrior in the East African country of Kenya

Africa is a big continent.

It has many countries, many people, and many different languages. The words we use to celebrate Kwanzaa come from the Swahili language. Swahili is spoken mostly in East and Central Africa, but you can hear it in places all over the world.

About 35 million people speak Swahili. If you wanted to greet someone in that language, you would say, "Jambo!"

"Hello!"

∧ *A U.S. postage stamp commemorates Kwanzaa.*

Before the celebration begins, we decorate our homes with the colors and symbols of Kwanzaa. The colors are red, green, and black. We use wall hangings, African cloth, and special artwork.

We make beautiful

things for Kwanzaa.

∧ In a California classroom,
children weave strips of
paper into mkeka mats.

< Marjorie Terrell displays
dolls dressed with lovely
African cloth in Plainfield,
New Jersey.

We can buy decorations, but it's more fun to make them ourselves. Creativity is one of the seven principles of Kwanzaa, so we use our imaginations.

In our decorations, we include

many important symbols of Kwanzaa. We put a mat, called an *mkeka,* on our tables. We arrange a basket filled with fruits and vegetables on the mkeka, to represent the harvest. Ears of corn are placed on the mat, one for each child in the family. The *kikombe cha umoja,* or unity cup, is placed there, too.

v *In Oakland, California, a boy places a lighted candle in a kinara.*

mkeka

Most important is the *kinara*, the special candleholder, and the seven candles it holds—one black, three red, and three green.

kikombe cha umoja

kinara

∧ *A father holds his daughter, who in turn holds the unity cup. It is usually filled with water—something pure from the earth.*

> *A woman celebrates Kwanzaa at home.*

We can't wait
for Kwanzaa!

> A gourd rattle

As Kwanzaa gets closer,

we practice drumming and dancing.
We buy or make gifts, called *zawadi,*
for our friends and families. We help
others make gifts, too. A parent, an
older brother or sister, or a friend
might show younger children how to
make drums and rattles and rainsticks,
colored necklaces, or woven mats.

Gifts can be given any time during
the week of Kwanzaa, but mostly we
wait until the last day. It's not easy to
be patient.

< *In Florida, Paige Armour shrieks with laughter
when a present is "stolen" from her by her
friend, Gloria Dover. Swapping food and gifts is
a traditional game in many parts of Africa.*

13

On the 26th of December,

we light the first candle of Kwanzaa. It is the center, black candle. The black candle stands for the unity of black people. Unity means standing together and helping each other.

Over the next six days we will light six more candles—three red and three green—one each day. The red candles on the left side represent our past. We remember our ancestors, many of whom were brought to this country as slaves. We think of their struggles and their triumphs. The green candles on the right stand for our hopes and dreams for the future.

> *Travis Holley lights the first candle of this Kwanzaa celebration in Linden, New Jersey.*

We celebrate
 with candles.

A family in South Pasadena, California, reads together during Kwanzaa.

Each day we light another candle.

We talk about the seven principles of Kwanzaa:

UMOJA (unity): Striving for togetherness with our families and communities.

KUJICHAGULIA (self-determination): Deciding for ourselves who we are, who we want to be, and what we want to do.

UJIMA (work and responsibility): Working together to build and strengthen our communities.

The seven principles

UJAMAA (cooperation): Building and supporting African-American stores and businesses and benefiting from them together.

NIA (purpose): Setting personal goals to make our communities strong.

KUUMBA (creativity): Thinking of ways to make our community and the world a better place.

IMANI (faith): Believing in ourselves, our communities, and the people around us.

∧ A mancala board

We gather together to sing,

dance, play drums, and celebrate our culture. Sometimes we play games. Grown-ups and children like to play *mancala,* a board game that is popular around the world. It is played with pebbles, beads, or seeds and can be played almost anywhere.

We gather together.

∧ *In New York City, people join hands in celebration of community and unity.*

< *Four children play mancala in East Africa.*

During Kwanzaa, we eat special foods. Some families use recipes passed from one generation to the next. We might have peanut soup or shrimp gumbo. Sometimes we have fried bananas, sweet potato pie, or coconut sweets.

fun

∧ African-American children perform a folk dance in the Bronx, New York.

friends

On the sixth day or night of the holiday, we have a great feast, called the Karamu. We dress in bright clothing to display the patterns and colors of Africa. We have drumming, music, and dance. We sing. We welcome as many people as we can. And we eat!

< Young men drum for the Kwanzaa feast of Karamu, which celebrates creativity. Drumming is a form of communication as well as celebration.

feast

January 1 is the last day
of Kwanzaa. It is a quieter time.
We have a farewell ceremony for
Kwanzaa. We greet the new year.
We focus on the things we have
learned. We give one another gifts.
We remember our roots and the
traditions of our ancestors. We
think of their struggles, and we
talk of our hopes for the future.

We remember

A girl in Washington, D.C., waits for her turn to dance in celebration of Kwanzaa.

our roots.

We wish for strength.

We wish to be united as one people and to work together to make the world better for those to come. We hope to preserve the good things in our lives and in our world.

We hope to make the world a better place.

> *In New York City, members of a dance company perform a traditional African dance.*

MORE ABOUT KWANZAA

Contents

Just the Facts

WHO CELEBRATES IT: African Americans and their friends and families.

WHAT: A holiday to celebrate African-American heritage, culture, achievements, and future.

WHEN: December 26 through January 1.

RITUAL: Lighting a candle each day, remembering the past, and celebrating the future. Drumming, dancing, making and giving gifts, feasting.

FOOD: A feast to celebrate harvest time. It includes everything from coconut milk and banana fritters to collard greens and sweet potato dishes.

> *A woman lights candles for Kwanzaa with her children in Toronto, Canada.*

Slavery

Most Africans were forced to come to America against their will. They came as slaves. Slaves were bought and sold. They were treated like possessions. Families were broken. People lived their whole lives without hope of freedom for themselves or their children.

Kwanzaa celebrates the need to know about the past and to create a more positive future. After the years of slavery, segregation, and the struggle for civil rights and justice, black people in the United States wanted to rediscover their roots and take pride in their African ancestry.

Kwanzaa celebrates the black community and the unity and triumph of black people.

< A rainstick displays the rich decorations of Africa.

Make a Rainstick

Clank clink, tap tap, shushhhh . . . These are some of the sounds you might hear from rainsticks and rattles during a Kwanzaa music and dance celebration. You can make very different sounds with them, depending on the container you use and what you put in it. Small dried pasta makes a *rat-a-tat-tat* sound, dried beans go *tap tap tap*, and rice makes a sort of *shushhhh*. You can use any kind of cardboard tube. Be creative!

YOU WILL NEED:

A cardboard tube (wrapping paper tubes are perfect!)
Waxed paper
Rubber bands
Grains of rice, pasta, or dried beans
Pushpin

1
Decorate the empty tube with African colors (red, green, and black), stickers, pictures, glitter—whatever you want.

2
Cover one end of the tube with waxed paper and attach the paper tightly with a rubber band.

3
Pour a handful of dried beans, rice, or pasta into the open end. Seal the opening with waxed paper and a rubber band.

4
Poke holes in the tube with the pushpin. Turn the tube very slowly or shake it quickly and listen to the different sounds you can make.

A piece of sweet potato pie, creamy and delicious.

Sweet Potato Pie

Recipes like this one for sweet potato pie are often handed down from one generation to the next. This family favorite is sweet and delicious. Be sure to have an adult help you at the stove.

INGREDIENTS:

2 large eggs
$\frac{1}{2}$ cup plus 2 tablespoons sugar
dash salt
$\frac{1}{2}$ teaspoon cinnamon
$\frac{1}{4}$ teaspoon allspice
$\frac{1}{8}$ teaspoon nutmeg
$\frac{1}{4}$ teaspoon lemon juice
$\frac{1}{2}$ teaspoon vanilla
$\frac{1}{2}$ cup heavy cream
$1\frac{1}{2}$ cups cooked, mashed sweet potatoes
1 unbaked pie shell

1. Preheat oven to 350°F.

2. Beat eggs well. Add sugar, salt, spices, lemon juice, and vanilla to the eggs. Mix thoroughly.

3. Add cream and stir.

4. Add mashed sweet potatoes and mix thoroughly.

5. Turn into pie shell and bake for 1 hour or until firm.

6. Let pie cool. Serve warm or cold.

Find Out More

BOOKS

Those with a star (*) are especially good for children.

*Brady, April A. *Kwanzaa Karamu: Cooking and Crafts for a Kwanzaa Feast.* Carolrhoda Books, 1995. Explains the origins of the holiday and provides recipes and crafts.

Grier, Ella. *Seven Days of Kwanzaa: How to Celebrate Them.* Sterling, 2005. A good overview of the Kwanzaa celebration day by day. Illustrated by John Ward.

Karenga, Maulana. *Kwanzaa: A Celebration of Family, Community, and Culture.* University of Sankore Press, 1997. By the creator of Kwanzaa.

*Marsh, Carole. *Kwanzaa: Activities, Crafts, Recipes, and More!* Gallopade International, 2003. Great for kids of all ages.

*Medearis, Angela Shelf. *Seven Spools of Thread: A Kwanzaa Story.* Albert Whitman and Company, 2000. A beautiful tale of seven brothers who overcome their differences. Illustrated with woodcuts by Daniel Minter.

*Morninghouse, Sundaira. *Habari Gani? What's the News?: A Kwanzaa Story.* Open Hand Publishers, 1992. An engagingly illustrated book to share with younger children. Illustrated by Jody Kim.

WEB SITES

Here are some fun sites full of ideas, crafts, recipes, and information:

childfun.com
For facts, crafts, and recipes, go to "Holidays" in the Site Menu and click on "Kwanzaa."

familyeducation.com
Type in "Kwanzaa" as the key word in the search engine, and follow the links for information and fun.

www.kaboose.com
Go to "Holidays and Fun" and click on "Kwanzaa" for an educational, kid-friendly site.

v Harold Anderson (left) and Jose Ferrer unveil the first Kwanzaa postage stamp in 1997, Harlem, New York City.

Glossary

Ancestry: Your family's background and history.

Imani (ee-MAH-nee): Faith.

Karamu (Ka-RAH-moo): A feast held on the seventh day of Kwanzaa.

Kikombe cha umoja (kee-KOHM-bee chah oo-MO-jah): The unity cup, which is passed from person to person during Kwanzaa.

Kinara (kee-NAH-rah): A candleholder for the seven candles of Kwanzaa.

Kujichagulia (koo-jee-chah-GOO-lee-ah): Self-determination.

Kuumba (koo-OOM-bah): Creativity.

Mkeka (em-KEH-kah): A mat or table covering.

Nguzo Saba (n-GU-zo SAH-bah): The seven principles of Kwanzaa.

Nia (NEE-ah): Purpose.

Ujamaa (oo-jah-MAH-ah): Cooperative economics.

Ujima (oo-JEE-mah): Collective work and responsibility.

Umoja (oo-MO-jah): Unity.

Where This Book's Photos Were Taken

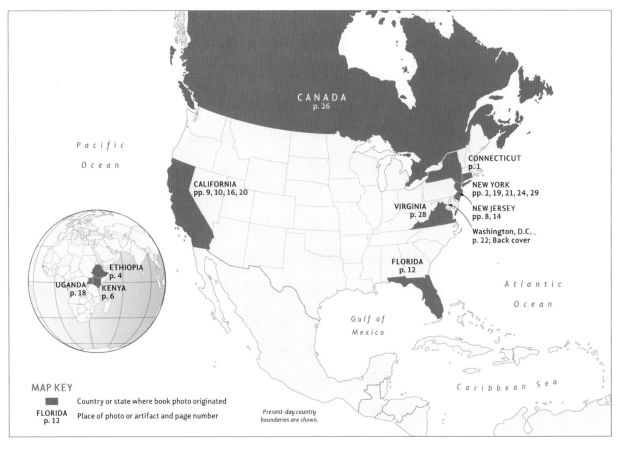

Kwanzaa: An African-American Holiday With Universal Appeal

by Keith A. Mayes, Ph.D.

Although Kwanzaa is not an African holiday, it was inspired by African culture and is based on African cultural practices. Kwanzaa was created in 1966 by Maulana Karenga and the Us organization in Los Angeles during the civil rights and black power movements that began in the 1950s and continued through the 1970s. The civil rights movement sought to eliminate segregation and discrimination in areas such as public accommodations, education, housing, and employment.

The black power movement, however, focused on the African-American quest for self-discovery and group identity. Searching for this identity from a new understanding of what it meant to be African and finding pride in blackness became its major preoccupation. Whereas civil rights is associated with the South, nonviolent direct action, and the strategies employed by Martin Luther King, Jr., black power highlighted an African past and an existence that transcended U.S. boundaries.

Kwanzaa is a prime example of African Americans' desire to discover their African heritage and reconnect with the continent of their ancestors. In fact, Kwanzaa is the product not of one individual but of an entire community. Kwanzaa would not be known to the world today if it were not for the black community in the late 1960s and early 1970s. In cities across the U.S., black social activists as well as apolitical African Americans embraced Kwanzaa and promoted the holiday in their homes, schools, and community centers.

Today, young people may be Kwanzaa's largest audience and most important constituents. Many black children have been introduced to Kwanzaa in their homes or schools, where the African side of African-American identity has been reinforced. Kwanzaa has rooted African-American children in their history and culture, providing them with a sense of belonging in the world. This sense of belonging not only means that black children have a holiday of their own, it also reinforces the idea that African Americans come from a people that have made significant contributions to human history and possess a glorious past. Kwanzaa's appeal to young people has much to do with posterity. Young people represent the future—their own future and the future of those not yet born. Not only are black youth heirs and custodians of Kwanzaa who can ensure the holiday's survival, but they are also the heirs and custodians of a brighter future for African Americans in general. This is what Kwanzaa speaks to.

Although Kwanzaa is grounded in black culture, the holiday's seven principles represent universal values that anyone can relate to. The principles of unity, self-determination, collective work and responsibility, cooperative economics, purpose, creativity, and faith are not "black" values—they are universal. Kwanzaa has transcended the boundaries of black America. The holiday is recognized by mainstream American society, and celebrations are held in major museums, libraries, and religious institutions across the U.S. and around the world.

Kwanzaa's growth and appeal beyond black America reflects the universality of its main components and symbols. Like other holidays, Kwanzaa is values oriented and driven, historically rooted, activities based, and youth focused—giving it a universal appeal. In this sense, the holiday represents the best of African-American culture, U.S. society, and humanity: unique, experimental, creative, improvisational, and put together from many parts.

Consultant Keith Mayes is an assistant professor in the Department of African-American and African Studies at the University of Minnesota. His writings include "Kwanzaa and the African-American Holiday Tradition" in American Holidays and National Days, *edited by Len Travers.*

For Renee

PICTURE CREDITS

Front cover: Mark Adams/ Taxi/ Getty Images; Back cover: Brendan Smialowski/ AFP/ Getty Images; Spine: Comstock; 1: Arnold Gold / New Haven Register / The Image Works; 2: Mario Tama/ Getty Images; 3 top: Hill Street Studios/Blend Images/Corbis; 3 bottom: Schomburg Center for Research in Black Culture/ The New York Public Library; 4-5: Gavin Hellier/ Robert Harding World Imagery/ Getty Images; 6-7: John Warburton-Lee; 8 top: USPS/ Associated Press; 8 bottom: Frank Conlon/ The Star-Ledger/ Corbis; 9: Kristopher Skinner/ Contra Costa Newspapers/ ZUMA Press; 10: Lonny Shavelson/ ZUMA Press; 11 top: Tom Wilson/ Taxi/ Getty Images; 11 bottom: Photo Network/ Alamy Ltd; 12-13: Amanda Voisard/ Palm Beach Post/ ZUMA Press; 13 right: Comstock; 14-15: Tim Farrell/ The Star-Ledger/ Corbis; 16: FoodPix/ Jupiter Images; 18 top: Kenneth Sponsler/ Shutterstock; 18 bottom: Bea Ahbeck/ Fremont Argus/ ZUMA Press;19: Jennifer Szymaszek/ Associated Press; 20: Kayte M. Deioma/ PhotoEdit Inc.; 21: James Leynse/ Corbis; 22-23: Brendan Smialowski/ AFP/ Getty Images; 24-25: Stephen Chernin/ Getty Images; 26: David Cooper/ Toronto Star/ ZUMA Press; 27: Sébastien Fortier/ iStockphoto.com; 28: Andrew Keegan and Mary Beth Oelkers-Keegan; 29: Bebeto Matthews/ Associated Press.

Library of Congress Cataloging-in-Publication Data
Otto, Carolyn.
 Celebrate Kwanzaa / Carolyn Otto; consultant, Keith A. Mayes.
   p. cm. —(Holidays around the world)
 ISBN 978-1-4263-0319-7 (trade) — ISBN 978-1-4263-0320-3 (library)
 1. Kwanzaa—Juvenile literature. 2. United States—Social life and customs—Juvenile literature. I. Title. GT4403.O88 2007
394.2612—dc22

2007041221

Series design by 3+Co. and Jim Hiscott.
The body text in the book is set in Mrs. Eaves.
The display text is Lisboa.
Printed in the United States of America

Front cover: These parents are teaching their daughter what the kinara candles stand for.
Back cover: African Heritage Dancers celebrate Kwanzaa at the Lincoln Theater in Washington, D.C.
Title page: A boy lights the candles during Kwanzaa.

Founded in 1888, the National Geographic Society is one of the largest nonprofit scientific and educational organizations in the world. It reaches more than 285 million people worldwide each month through its official journal, NATIONAL GEOGRAPHIC, and its four other magazines; the National Geographic Channel; television documentaries; radio programs; films; books; videos and DVDs; maps; and interactive media. National Geographic has funded more than 8,000 scientific research projects and supports an education program combating geographic illiteracy.

For more information, please call 1-800-NGS LINE (647-5463) or write to the following address:

National Geographic Society
1145 17th Street N.W.
Washington, D.C. 20036-4688 U.S.A.

Visit us online at www.nationalgeographic.com/books

For information about special discounts for bulk purchases, please contact National Geographic Books Special Sales: ngspecsales@ngs.org. For rights or permissions inquiries, please contact National Geographic Books Subsidiary Rights: ngbookrights@ngs.org

PUBLISHED BY THE NATIONAL GEOGRAPHIC SOCIETY

John M. Fahey, Jr., *President and Chief Executive Officer*
Gilbert M. Grosvenor, *Chairman of the Board*
Tim T. Kelly, *President, Global Media Group*
Nina D. Hoffman, *Executive Vice President; President, Book Publishing Group*

STAFF FOR THIS BOOK

Nancy Laties Feresten, *Vice President, Editor-in-Chief of Children's Books*
Bea Jackson, *Design and Illustrations Director, Children's Books*
Amy Shields, *Executive Editor, Children's Books*
Mary Beth Oelkers-Keegan, *Project Editor*
Lori Epstein, *Illustrations Editor*
Melissa Brown, *Project Designer*
Carl Mehler, *Director of Maps*
Priyanka Lamichhane, *Assistant Editor*
Rebecca Baines, *Editorial Assistant*
Rachel Armor, *Editorial Intern*
Jennifer A. Thornton, *Managing Editor*
Gary Colbert, *Production Director*
Lewis R. Bassford, *Production Manager*
Maryclare Tracy, Nicole Elliott, *Manufacturing Managers*
Susan E. Borke, *Senior Vice President and Deputy General Counsel*

ACKNOWLEDGMENTS

Many thanks to Dr. Keith Mayes for his insightful editorial comments and powerful note. To Tammi Hawes, another teacher whose influence upon our children is profound. And to Nancy, Mary Beth, and Amy, for helping me get things right.